Satisfied With Not Being Satisfied Workbook

Sandra DeShawn Cavette

HATCHBACK Publishing
Genesee Michigan

Satisfied With Not Being Satisfied Workbook
©2019 Sandra DeShawn Cavette.

All Rights Reserved. No portion of this book may be reproduced, stored in a retrieval system, or transmitted in any form or by any means – electronic mechanical, photocopy or other – except for brief quotation in printed review, without the prior permission of the author or publisher.

All Scripture taken from Biblegateway the King James Version Public Domain no permission necessary.
www.biblegateway.com

Published by: HATCHBACK Publishing
                    Genesee, Michigan 48437
                    Since 2005

ISBN 978-1-948708-35-7

Printed in the United States of America
10 9 8 7 6 5 4 3 2 1

For Worldwide Distribution

Table Of Contents

Introduction - Pleasing People or Pleasing God...5

Eye Opener...7

Leaving The Past...9

Marriage-Get In The Boat - Try Something New...12

Your Spouse - Your Friend...15

Forgiveness...18

Know Your Worth...22

Relationships...25

Mentor/Mentee...30

Healthy Nuts and Seeds...32

Knowing Your Purpose...35

We Are The Teacher- Our Children...37

Prayer...40

Music And The Moment...42

Your Heart...44

Your Mind...49

Reading...52

Life Changers...55

Words Have Power...57

The Pastor's Wife...59

Technology & Social Media...62

Reminiscing/The Good Old Days...64

Talking Clay- A Conversation With God...66

Satisfied With The Wrong Man...68

Introduction

Pleasing People or Pleasing God

Many of us allow people, obstacles and circumstances to stop us from achieving our goals. This happens to people often. If we know what we want, where we want to go and who we want to be with are we settling for what is easy and convenient?

_____
_____
_____
_____

You are going to please someone. Are you going to please God or please others; family, friends, favorites, co-workers, spouse, significant others?

_____
_____
_____

What are your priorities?

_____
_____
_____
_____
_____
_____
_____

Are you a priority to the people you make a priority?_____

Is God a priority?_____

Eye Opener

"A Jesus Reality Check" happens after you check with all your sources and you see that people cannot help you. You will know that God and God alone is your source.

What was your Eye Opener?

_____
_____
_____
_____
_____
_____
_____
_____
_____
_____

How did you handle it?

_____
_____
_____
_____
_____
_____
_____
_____

Did you allow God to take control or did you handle it yourself? _____

How can you apply (Romans 8:28, James 5:16, Isaiah 40:31)

_____
_____
_____
_____
_____
_____
_____
_____
_____
_____
_____
_____
_____
_____

Leaving The Past

PAST= Problems, Attitudes, Situations and Things

How did you handle your problems, attitudes, and situations in the past?

_____
_____
_____
_____
_____
_____
_____
_____
_____

How does your past affect you today?

_____
_____
_____
_____
_____
_____
_____
_____
_____

How has God changed the way you deal with your past?

_____
_____
_____
_____
_____
_____

Are you still holding on to something from the past?_____
Why?_____

_____
_____
_____
_____
_____
_____

See (2 Corinthians 5:17; Isaiah 43:18; Philippians 3:13-14)

_____
_____
_____
_____
_____
_____
_____
_____
_____
_____

What do you need to do to move forward?

_____
_____
_____
_____
_____
_____
_____
_____
_____

Marriage- Get In the Boat (Try Something New)

It is imperative to stay in touch with what is going on in your spouse's life.

Are you making your mate a daily priority? _____

When was the last time you did something your mate wanted to do? What was it?
_____
_____
_____
_____
_____
_____
_____
_____
_____
_____

Are you willing to try something new?
_____
_____
_____

Do you pray for your spouse daily, and spend quality time together?
_____
_____
_____

Genesis 2:22-24, Proverbs 5:18-19, Proverbs 18:22, Proverbs 31:10, Ephesians 5:22-33, Colossians 3:18-19

_____
_____
_____
_____
_____
_____
_____
_____
_____
_____
_____
_____
_____
_____
_____
_____
_____
_____
_____
_____
_____
_____

What does it mean to be a husband/wife?

_____
_____
_____

What improvements do you need to make to have a better marriage?

Your Spouse-Your Friend

It's a beautiful thing for your spouse to be your best friend, lover, and soul mate. Is your spouse your best friend?

_____
_____
_____
_____

Do you feel like it is important to have other friends besides your spouse?

_____
_____
_____
_____
_____

Do you and your spouse communicate well? _____

If not, what do you need to do to improve your communication?

_____
_____
_____
_____
_____
_____
_____
_____

If there is an issue/problem in your marriage do you talk about it right away or do you see if it works itself out?

_____
_____
_____
_____
_____

What do you and your spouse need to do to improve your marriage?

_____
_____
_____
_____
_____
_____
_____
_____
_____
_____
_____
_____

Do you make your spouse's needs a priority?

_____
_____

Do you make time for your spouse daily, weekly, and monthly?

_____
_____
_____

Is intimacy an important part of your marriage?

_____
_____
_____
_____
_____
_____
_____

Forgiveness

Forgiveness may be one of the most psychological and emotional experiences you will ever encounter in life. Whether you are asked to forgive someone, seeking forgiveness or simply trying to forgive yourself, forgiveness is necessary.

Are you able to forgive people who have offended you?
_____
_____
_____

Do you forgive people quickly or does it take a long time?
_____
_____
_____
_____
_____

Do you think forgiving is really necessary?
_____
_____
_____

Ephesians 4:32, 1 John 1:9, Mark 11:25, Matthew 6:14-15
_____
_____
_____
_____
_____
_____

_____
_____
_____
_____
_____
_____
_____
_____
_____

How many times are we to forgive? Matthew 18:22-23
How do we apply this scripture?

_____
_____
_____
_____
_____
_____
_____

How does unforgiveness affect us?

_____
_____
_____
_____
_____
_____
_____

What do you do when you forgive someone and they don't want to forgive you?

_____
_____
_____
_____
_____
_____
_____

What are some steps that should be taken to begin the forgiveness process?

_____
_____
_____
_____
_____
_____
_____

If you or your spouse keeps bringing up an issue from your past, have you really forgiven?

_____
_____
_____
_____
_____
_____
_____

Is it possible to forgive and forget?

_____
_____
_____
_____
_____
_____

Know Your Worth

In our lives when we will feel discouraged, depressed, beat down, alone, stressed and even filled with doubt on how God sees us, satan likes to attack our mind making us think that we have no self-worth and that God does not value us. At other times as Christians we need reminders of how God sees us with tremendous value. We are fearful and wondrously made… (Psalms 139:14)

Do you really know your worth?

_____
_____
_____
_____
_____
_____

Read Jeremiah 29:11 Explain

_____
_____
_____
_____
_____
_____

Are you allowing God to use you for His service?

_____
_____
_____

What is hindering you from allowing God to use you?

_____
_____
_____
_____
_____
_____

Romans 5:8: Matthew 16:26; Romans 3:23

_____
_____
_____
_____
_____
_____
_____
_____
_____
_____
_____
_____

God is concerned about you. He even knows how many hairs are on your head.

(Luke 12:7) How would you apply this scripture to your life?

_____
_____
_____
_____
_____
_____
_____

Our value is based upon the gifts with which God has equipped us to live for Him and the position that we have in Christ. Thank you Lord for giving us worth! No man can put a value on our worth! When you know your worth, you will not allow anyone to make you feel worthless!

Relationships

We have different relationships with people. Some people we admire, adore, tolerate, avoid, and some we despise. God desires for us to have a relationship with Him. Sin has caused our relationship to be broken with God.

Broken relationship with God

Isaiah 53:6

_____
_____
_____
_____
_____

John 3:19-20: Ephesians 2:1-2

_____
_____
_____
_____
_____

Restored Relationship with God

John 3:16, John14:6

_____
_____
_____
_____
_____

Everlasting Relationship with God

Hebrews 13:5; 1 John 5:13

_____
_____
_____
_____
_____
_____
_____
_____
_____

What do you want out of the relationships you are currently involved in?

_____
_____
_____
_____

Are you allowing issues from the past to hinder you from a new relationship?

_____
_____
_____
_____
_____

What improvements do you need to make to have better relationships? (ex. communication, trust, forgiveness, jealousy, selfishness, anger, lying)?

_____
_____
_____
_____
_____
_____

You cannot change the other person but you can make changes to your behavior.

Communication is one of the areas where there are breakdowns in relationships. What are some behaviors you can do to communicate more effectively?

_____
_____
_____
_____
_____

How do you effectively deal with conflict?

_____
_____
_____
_____
_____

Are you willing to compromise in your relationship?

_____
_____

Communication is one key element in any relationship. Don't assume you know what other people want. When you practice expressing your needs you are able to keep the lines of communication clear. Communication requires talking and listening, and most people find it easier to talk than to actively listen.

Do you consider yourself a good communicator?

_____
_____
_____

Do you tend to listen more or talk more when you are communicating?

_____
_____
_____

The greatest communicators are known to be first and foremost great listeners.

Do you agree with this statement?

_____
_____
_____

Have you've experienced having a conversation with someone and they dominated the conversation and you weren't able to speak?

_____
_____
_____
_____

How did that make you feel?

_____
_____
_____
_____
_____
_____

Mentor/Mentee

A mentor can help the mentee improve their skills and abilities through assessment, observation, modeling and guidance. Before any mentoring can take place a relationship must be established.

Are you a mentor or mentee?
_____
_____
_____

If so how has this relationship impacted your life?
_____
_____
_____
_____
_____

Have you encountered any problems with your mentor/mentee?
_____
_____
_____
_____

Are you willing to be a mentor/mentee to another others?
_____
_____
_____
_____

Do you have a spiritual mentor?
_____
_____
_____

Are you willing to allow them to help you grow spiritually?
_____
_____
_____

Are you willing to be accountable to your mentor/mentee?
_____
_____
_____

Some examples of mentor/mentee relationships are Moses/Joshua, and Ruth and Naomi. What are some examples of wisdom you received from your mentor/mentee?
_____
_____
_____
_____
_____
_____
_____

If you don't have a mentor I suggest you experience this relationship.

Healthy Nuts And Seeds

Seeds and nuts make up an important part of a healthy diet. Both of these foods help you to reach your recommended intake of protein per day and count toward your daily fat allowance. Nuts and seeds provide a source of dietary fiber. It is always best to check with your doctor before changing your eating habits.

Are you satisfied with your spiritual, physical, and mental health?
_____
_____
_____
_____
_____
_____
_____
_____
_____

Do you eat nuts and seeds as part of your regular diet?
_____
_____
_____

Are you willing to try to add nuts and seeds to your diet?
_____
_____
_____

People who consume nuts regularly tend to weigh less than those who rarely eat nuts, as well as face a lower risk for future weight gain.

What nuts and seeds do you like?
_____
_____
_____

Are you willing to try some new seeds and nuts? _____

Do you have a plan to help you eat healthier?
_____
_____
_____
_____
_____

Is it certain things that trigger you to eat unhealthy foods?
_____
_____
_____
_____
_____

Has weight gain/loss been a struggle for you?
_____
_____
_____
_____

Do you take care of your physical man as well as you do your spiritual man?

_____
_____
_____

Are you up to date on your doctor's visits? _____

Do you look out for others and neglect taking proper care of yourself?

_____
_____

What changes can you make today that will help you become healthier?

_____
_____
_____
_____

1 Corinthians 3:16; 6:19

_____
_____
_____
_____
_____
_____
_____

A little change in your eating habits can make a big impact. Your body is the temple. We only have one so let's take better care of ourselves. I encourage you to make the proper changes to become a healthier you.

Knowing Your Purpose

Many times when we are seeking God's will, we want to know every step before it happens. We all know God doesn't work like that. When you allow God to take complete control, not only will the Lord show you which direction you are to move; He will also reveal the appropriate time and method to take.

Do you know what God's purpose is for your life?

_____
_____
_____
_____
_____
_____
_____

Do you know your spiritual gifts and talents?

_____
_____
_____
_____
_____
_____
_____

What is your passion?
_____
_____
_____
_____
_____

Jonah was running from the will of God (Jonah 1:1-17).
Are you allowing God to lead you in the direction He has for your life?
_____
_____
_____
_____

2 Corinthians 5:7, Isaiah 55:8
_____
_____
_____
_____
_____
_____
_____
_____
_____
_____
_____
_____

We Are The Teacher - Our Children

Our society has sex in the forefront of everything you see on a daily basis. There was a time when people respected their bodies. Now people show everything to everyone. It's left up to us to teach the young people about respecting themselves and others. It is the responsibility of the parents to raise their own children. You can tell them what to do but they are modeling the behaviors they see.

What does being a teacher/role model mean to you?

_____
_____
_____
_____
_____

Proverbs 22:6

_____
_____
_____
_____
_____

The children are watching their parent's attitudes, actions and behaviors. Are you exemplifying Christ like behavior? _____

Are you teaching or have you given your children biblical principles to have a productive walk with God?

_____
_____
_____
_____

Were you taught biblical principles when you were a youth?

_____
_____
_____
_____

What are some Christian values that you feel should be taught to children today?

_____
_____
_____

What do you need to do to eradicate negative behaviors in your children?

_____
_____
_____
_____
_____
_____

Do you pray for your children daily?

_____
_____
_____

Have you taught your children to seek God for direction in their lives?

_____
_____
_____
_____
_____

Deuteronomy 4:9-10, Proverbs 23:13-14, Proverbs 29:15,17, Ephesians 6:4

_____
_____
_____
_____
_____
_____
_____
_____

Prayer

Prayer is essential to growing spiritual and knowing God. The power of prayer should never be underestimated. When you pray it is imperative that you believe that God has the power to change your circumstances.

Do you have a daily prayer life?
_____
_____
_____
_____

Do you believe God answers your prayers?
_____
_____
_____
_____
_____

Are you taking control of the obstacles and problems you are facing or are you giving God a chance to work situations out for you?
_____
_____
_____
_____
_____

James 5:16, 2 Chronicles 7:14, Matthew 26:41, Philippians 4:6

_____
_____
_____
_____
_____
_____
_____
_____
_____
_____

Don't wait until your prayer is answered to praise Him.
Praise Him in advance for breakthrough.

Music And The Moment

Music is a pervasive part of our culture today. It is powerful and has a definite impact in most, if not all aspects of our lives. Music can unlock a door into your soul and take your mind to another place. It can motivate you positively or negatively.

Is there certain songs you listen to for your mood to change?

_____
_____
_____
_____

Is worship and praise part of your Christian walk?

_____
_____
_____
_____

How important is music in your life?

_____
_____
_____
_____
_____
_____
_____

2 Chronicles 5:12-13, Psalms 150: 1-6, 1 Samuel 16:23, Colossians 3:16

_____
_____
_____
_____
_____
_____
_____
_____
_____
_____

The next time we listen to music. Think about how it is used to influence us, set the atmosphere for whatever our hearts desire, and affect our mentality.

Your Heart

God requires believers to possess a spiritual heart that has been transformed from the sinful nature. During this process you have repented of your sins and allowed God to humble you and let the Holy Spirit lead you. This regenerated heart fears God, trusts Him, is faithful and obedient to His will.

The Bible says in Jeremiah 29:17 "The heart is deceitful above all things, and desperately wicked: who can know it?" We tend to go astray every time we follow our heart and not follow the directions of the Lord.

Man looks at the outward appearance but the Lord looks at the heart..."
(1 Samuel 16:7)

How can you tell if you are allowing God to work in your heart?

_____
_____
_____
_____
_____

Is there something you are dealing with in your heart that you have not allowed God to change?

_____
_____
_____
_____
_____

How do you deal with people who have broken your heart in the past?
_____
_____
_____
_____
_____
_____

Do you usually follow what your mind wants to do or what your heart wants to do?
_____
_____
_____
_____
_____
_____

With all your heart… Proverbs 3:5-6
_____
_____
_____
_____

Treasure and your heart… Matthew 6:21
_____
_____
_____
_____

Guard your heart... Proverbs 4:23

_____
_____
_____
_____
_____

Give me your heart... Proverbs 23:26

_____
_____
_____
_____
_____

A pure heart... Psalms 51:10

_____
_____
_____
_____
_____

Strength of my heart... Psalms 73:26

_____
_____
_____
_____
_____

Troubled heart... John 14:27

_____
_____
_____

_____
_____

Desires of your heart... Psalms 37:4
_____
_____
_____
_____

With all my heart... Psalms 9:1
_____
_____
_____
_____

Broken heart... Psalms 34:18
_____
_____
_____
_____

Pure in heart... Matthew 5:8
_____
_____
_____
_____

Meditation of my heart... Psalms 19:14

_____
_____
_____
_____
_____

There are different kinds of hearts examples (giving, kind, broken, harden, pure). What kind of heart do you possess?

_____
_____
_____
_____
_____

Your Mind

Believers should possess a new mind, transformed thinking, and thoughts to direct our spiritual, mental, and physical behavior. Our thoughts influence every action we take. God wants us to think on spiritual things that are pleasing to Him.

What kinds of thoughts do you usually have?
Example (positive, negative, worrying, spiritual, etc.)

_____
_____
_____
_____
_____
_____
_____
_____
_____
_____

What is your process to change your negative thoughts into positive thoughts?

_____
_____
_____
_____
_____
_____

_____
_____
_____
_____
_____
_____

How has renewed thinking helped you to have a more peaceful lifestyle?

_____
_____
_____
_____
_____

Do you worry about things you have no control over?

_____
_____
_____
_____

Romans 12:1-2 Renewing of your mind

_____
_____
_____
_____

Philippians 2:5   Let this mind

_____
_____
_____
_____
_____

Philippians 4:8   Think on these things

_____
_____
_____
_____
_____

Isaiah 26:3   Mind stayed on thee

_____
_____
_____
_____
_____

Reading

Reading is an excellent way to gain knowledge, improve your quality of life, keep your mind stimulated, and give you insight in new areas of your life. Studies have shown a way to possibly even prevent or slow the progress of Alzheimer's and Dementia, you must keep your brain engaged and active. Reading Christian books can also add depth to your spiritual life.

What books do you read to enhance your knowledge of God's Word?

___

Are you an avid reader?

___

How has reading increased your knowledge?

___

Reading helps people release stress and can take your mind to another place. What books have you read that seem to help you relax from the pressures of life?

_____
_____
_____
_____

Scripture given by inspiration   2 Timothy 3:16-17

_____
_____
_____
_____

The Word is a lamp Psalms 119:105

_____
_____
_____
_____

Every Word   Matthew 4:4

_____
_____
_____
_____

Word quick and powerful   Hebrews 4:12

_____
_____
_____
_____
_____

The Beginning John 1:1

_____
_____
_____
_____
_____

Words will not pass away Matthew 24:35

_____
_____
_____
_____
_____

Life Changers

We have people who we meet and have an immediate connection. The more we talk to them, it seems like we have known them all our lives. Some of these people are life changers. Meeting people with all types of personalities can be challenging. Romans 12:18 states, "If it be possible, as much as lieth in you, live peaceably with all men."

Who are some of the people who have made a positive impact in your life?

Do these people know how they have influence your life?

_____
_____
_____
_____
_____

Which of the sixteen personality traits can you relate to in the book that has been a life changer for you? Praying One, Dedicated Friend, Happy One, Needful One, Event Crasher, Boss Hog, Late One, Solo One, Twenty- Four Hundred/Self Righteous, Continual Complainer, One Up On You, Nice-Nasty, Can't Get It Right, Run and Tell That, Lying/ Thief, Two to Ten

_____
_____
_____
_____
_____

Trouble   John 14:1

_____
_____
_____
_____
_____

Ecclesiastes 3:1-8

_____
_____
_____
_____
_____

Psalms 23:1-6

_____
_____
_____
_____
_____

God is so good. He allows us to go through life lessons for us to learn and grow. If we don't learn our lesson the first time, God will keep taking us through the process until we learn. Every step we take is taking us closer to our DESTINY! Thank God for being with us through this life-changing experience.

Words Have Power

We speak countless words everyday, and pay little attention to what we are really saying.(Matthew 12:34) says "Out of the abundance of the heart the mouth speaks"...). It is important to realize that we are establishing our world by the words that we speak. With God living on the inside of you, your heart will be changed and you can make a total transformation of your words, thoughts, and your destiny.

Are you cautious about the words you speak?

_____
_____
_____
_____
_____

Are you speaking life or death into your situations?

_____
_____
_____
_____
_____

How has speaking life changed your situations?

_____
_____
_____
_____
_____

God wants you to be successful. What strategies do you use to allow your words to line up with God's plan for your life?

_____
_____
_____
_____
_____

Seek the kingdom first Matthew 6:33

_____
_____
_____
_____
_____

Every good gift James 1:17

_____
_____
_____
_____
_____

Life and death Proverbs 18:21

_____
_____
_____
_____
_____

Let us pay closer attention to the words we speak. Like the saying says "If we can't say anything positive it is best not to say anything. Our lives depend on it!

The Pastor's Wife

I've experienced triumphs, tests, celebrations, tears, accomplishments, trials, struggles, heartaches, and joys of being a wife of a pastor. I want to encourage every pastor's wife as we continue to walk in our calling. We are unique and God has equipped us for this journey. Buckle up and enjoy the ride!

If you are a Pastor's wife, do you have a good support system for your spiritual needs?

_____
_____
_____
_____
_____

What do you do to keep a healthy balance with the church, family, home, and work?

_____
_____
_____
_____
_____

Do you feel at times you are not getting enough quality time for yourself?

_____
_____
_____
_____
_____

Are you struggling to keep everyone satisfied (God, yourself, husband, children, church)?

_____
_____
_____
_____
_____

Has being a Pastor's wife been a blessing to you?

_____
_____
_____
_____
_____

How do you handle the demands this position has put on your marriage?

_____
_____
_____
_____
_____

Do you and your spouse have quality time together that does not involve church?

_____
_____
_____
_____
_____

Do your children feel like they have quality time with you and their dad (The Pastor)?

_____
_____
_____
_____
_____

Children are the heritage Psalms 127:3-5

_____
_____
_____
_____
_____

A wife a good thing   Proverbs 18:22

_____
_____
_____
_____
_____

Let God mold you into the Pastor's wife He has called you to be not what other people think you should be. Walk in your calling and let God be pleased with the service you give.

Technology and Social Media

Social networks can help your business, ministry or life in a variety of ways. Traditional marketing mediums such as television commercials, radio, and print are being used. However, with social media, you can connect with targeted customers, family, friends, church and group members for free.

How are you allowing social media to be a tool to be a marketing strategy to assist you and your ministry?

_____
_____
_____
_____
_____

Is social media and technology an important aspect of your life?

_____
_____
_____
_____
_____

Has social media and technology been a barrier for you to be successful?

_____
_____
_____
_____
_____

Are you staying abreast of the new trends and changing in technology?

_____
_____
_____
_____
_____

As long as we live we are changing. Change is all around us daily. If we don't change a change is going to come anyway. Don't find yourself walking on the Oregon Trail because you don't want to jump on the information highway!

Reminiscing/The Good Old Days

We all can look back and reminisce about things we have experienced in our pasts. One thing that can be acknowledged is we could not have made it this far without God. God has brought us through many things. Having biblical principles taught to me at an early age made a huge impact in my life. I find myself teaching my children the wisdom that was imparted to me.

What wisdom are you teaching the people you encounter to aid them in being better?

_____
_____
_____
_____
_____

Read Deuteronomy Chapter 6. How can you apply this today?

_____
_____
_____
_____
_____

What scriptures, words of advice, experiences, or testimonies, are you willing to share to help others?

_____
_____
_____
_____
_____

What are three "old school" sayings, (words of wisdom) that has resonated in your life?

_____
_____
_____
_____
_____

You can help someone who is willing to learn. If a person is not willing to learn because they think they already know, they cannot be helped. We used to call this person a "know it all". How can having this attitude deter from becoming the person God has destined us to be?

We are to impart wisdom in the next generation. Everyone can work together if we humble ourselves and allow God to teach us. We can all learn something from each other!

Talking Clay - A Conversation With God

God is the potter and we are the clay. (Isaiah 64:8) We are fearfully and wonderfully made. (Psalms 139:14) Just like a potter takes a piece of clay and rolls it, stretches it, flips it and turns it, that is what the Lord wants to do in our lives.

God knows the plans He has for our lives. It is usually not the same plans we have.

Are you allowing God to mold you into His Divine masterpiece?
_____
_____
_____
_____
_____

How do you recognize and know that it is God's voice speaking to you?
_____
_____
_____
_____
_____

Read (Jonah 1:1-3) How do handle being obedient to God when you want to do something different?
_____
_____
_____
_____
_____

Give an example of how being obedient to God has helped you to become the person God wants you to be spiritually and naturally?

_____
_____
_____
_____
_____

Let God turn what was just a dull and dingy lump of clay into a designer's masterpiece. God will mend every broken piece in your life. Will you surrender your will and say yes?

_____
_____
_____
_____
_____
_____

Satisfied With the Wrong Man

Love is one of the greatest gifts that God has given us. With that being said, I have encountered countless women that continue to stay in relationships that are detrimental, dangerous, unfulfilling, unhappy and depressing. Ladies it's time to let go of every stronghold that it stifling you. If you don't allow God to take control of every area of your life you will end up, lonely, depressed, stressed and unsatisfied.

Are you in a happy relationship with the man God has made just for you (your husband) not someone else's?

_____
_____
_____
_____
_____

Are you allowing yourself to be a side chick? (the other woman)

_____
_____
_____
_____
_____

If you are not the wife, *you are number* two, five, ten or whatever place you are allowing yourself to be. Why are you satisfied with being an option, because you are definitely not a priority?

_____
_____
_____
_____
_____

Do you know what you want your God fearing man (husband) to be like?

_____
_____
_____
_____
_____

Are you in a relationship with someone who has excuses as to why he can't, or won't marry you?

_____
_____
_____
_____
_____

Are you tired of being lied to, played on and treated like you have no worth?

_____
_____
_____
_____
_____

Do you always end up picking the wrong man?

_____
_____
_____
_____
_____

Are you ready and willing for God to bless you with the man of your dreams?

_____
_____
_____
_____
_____

While you are waiting on the Lord to bless you with your husband you have work to do to be the wife he needs you to be.

What do you need to do to be prepared for your husband?

_____
_____
_____
_____
_____

If you keep allowing yourself to be second you will never be number one. People treat you the way you allow them to treat you. If you allow a man to get the benefits of a wife without the title, you will always end up brokenhearted.

www.ingramcontent.com/pod-product-compliance
Lightning Source LLC
Chambersburg PA
CBHW081636040426
42449CB00014B/3339